# CAMPFIRE SONGS for ACOUSTIC GUITAR

BY MAURICE TANI

Publisher: Lyzy Lusterman
Editor: Adam Perlmutter
Managing Editor: Stephanie Campos Dal Broi
Design and Production: Joey Lusterman

ISBN 978-1-936604-46-3

This book was produced by
String Letter Publishing, Inc.
941 Marina Way South, Suite E, Richmond, CA 94804
(510) 215-0010;
Stringletter.com

# CONTENTS

**4** INTRODUCTION    **6** NOTATION GUIDE    **80** ABOUT THE AUTHOR

**11** ARE YOU LONESOME TONIGHT?

**14** THE BALLAD OF CASEY JONES

**18** BEAUTIFUL DREAMER

**20** DECK THE HALLS

**22** DRUNKEN SAILOR

**24** HOME ON THE RANGE

**26** HOUSE OF THE RISING SUN

**29** I'M SITTING ON TOP OF THE WORLD

**33** IT HAD TO BE YOU

**36** JENNY JENKINS

**38** JOHN HENRY

**42** LET ME CALL YOU SWEETHEART

**44** LOW BRIDGE, EVERYBODY DOWN

**46** MANHATTAN

**51** MY BONNIE LIES OVER THE OCEAN

**54** OH SHENANDOAH

**56** ON TOP OF OLD SMOKY

**58** RAGTIME COWBOY JOE

**62** RED RIVER VALLEY

**64** STEALIN'

**66** STREETS OF LAREDO

**70** THIS LITTLE LIGHT OF MINE

**72** TOM DOOLEY

**74** TONIGHT YOU BELONG TO ME

**77** WHAT'LL I DO

# INTRODUCTION

We call them campfire songs, but perhaps that's a bit simplistic. The label might bring to mind images of friends gathered around a warm fire, its flickering glow illuminating their faces as they sing and strum an acoustic guitar under the starry skies of the great outdoors—a romantic picture I'll make no attempt to dispel as I add to it.

Traditionally, these were the songs of the Old West sung by cowboys out on the open range or folk songs sung on the front porches of Appalachia—the early roots of Americana, modern blues, and country music. In more recent times, they were songs generations of kids grew up singing at summer camp while toasting marshmallows and hot dogs on long sticks. These were usually fairly simple tunes, played using open cowboy chords, making them particularly suitable for beginning players.

Of course, there is also plenty of familiar, and less rustic, repertoire that works well as campfire songs. For the purposes of this book, as a collection intended for acoustic guitar enthusiasts, we have broadened the scope to include selections that fit the basic mission statement of familiar songs that can be sung casually by groups of friends, but push the envelope of basic folk chords a bit.

Some of these songs hail from the early Great American Songbook. These are selections that became popular after the advent of recording and radio and have weathered cycles of obscurity and familiarity over generations of popular music.

As the times have changed, the styles, and often lyrics to these songs have changed to suit the day. Many of these songs have been recorded in a wide array of styles from simple folk to big band jazz and rock 'n' roll. I've generally tried to stay closer to the original versions of the songs, sometimes pulling from several versions to create an easy, single-guitar arrangement.

But while our focus is at the easy end of the difficulty scale, this book is for guitarists of all levels. I encourage you to first learn and play these songs and then make them your own. The simple arrangements can be taken as a starting point to create your own version of a classic song. Do a little digging online and explore other versions of the songs—there are many. Combine the elements you like and create the version that's best for you.

As a guitarist and singer-songwriter, I've really enjoyed learning—and learning about—these songs. I've come away from each one with something absorbed that eventually manifests in my playing, writing, or appreciation. These classic songs have stood the test of time and they still have something to give anyone who wants to take a crack at them.

So, enjoy! My hope is you may find that, regardless of whether you're inside or out, or whether you're with friends or alone, these songs are very satisfying to play even if there are no flashlights, ghost stories, or mosquito repellent involved.

—Maurice Tani

# VIDEO LESSONS

Each song includes an accompanying video lesson with Maurice Tani.

Go to **store.AcousticGuitar.com/campfirevideo** to download your videos.

Music is a language and, like many languages, has a written form. In order to be literate, one must become familiar with what each character and symbol represent.

Guitarists use several types of notation, including standard notation, tablature, and chord diagrams. Standard notation is a universal system in Western music. Becoming competent with standard notation will allow you to share and play music with almost any other instrument. Tablature is a notation system exclusively for stringed instruments with frets—like guitar and ukulele—that shows you what strings and frets to play to achieve the desired pitches. Chord diagrams use a graphic representation of the fretboard to show chord shapes on fretted instruments. Here's a primer on how to read these types of notation.

## STANDARD NOTATION

Standard notation is written on a five-line staff. Notes are written in alphabetical order from A to G. Every time you pass a G note, the sequence of notes repeats, starting with A.

The duration of a note is depicted by note head, stem, and flag. Though the number of beats each note represents will vary depending on the meter, the relations between note durations remain the same: a whole note ( o ) is double the length of a half note ( ♩ ). A half note is double the length of a quarter note ( ♩ ). A quarter note is double the length of an eighth note ( ♪ ). An eighth note is double the length of a sixteenth note ( ♫ ). And so on. You'll notice each time a flag gets added, the note duration halves.

The numbers that follow the clef (4/4, 3/4, 6/8, etc.) or **C** shown at the beginning of a piece of music denote the time signature. The top number tells you how many beats are in each measure, and the bottom number indicates the rhythmic value of each beat (4 equals a quarter note, 8 equals an eighth note, 16 equals a sixteenth note, and 2 equals a half note).

The most common time signature is 4/4, which signifies four quarter notes per measure and is sometimes designated with the symbol **C** (for common time). The symbol **₵** stands for cut time (2/2).

## TABLATURE

In tablature, the six horizontal lines represent the six strings of the guitar, low to high, as on the guitar. The numbers refer to fret numbers on the indicated string.

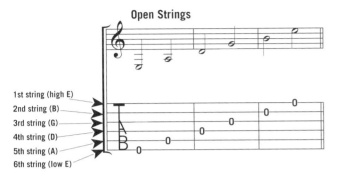

## FINGERINGS

Fingerings are indicated with small numbers and letters in the notation. Fretting-hand fingering is expressed as 1 for the index finger, 2 the middle, 3 the ring, 4 the pinky, and *T* the thumb. Picking-hand fingering is conveyed by *i* for the index finger, *m* the middle, *a* the ring, *c* the pinky, and *p* the thumb.

## STRUMMING AND PICKING

In music played with a flatpick, downstrokes (toward the floor) and upstrokes (toward the ceiling) are shown as follows. Slashes in the notation and tablature indicate a strum through the previously played chord.

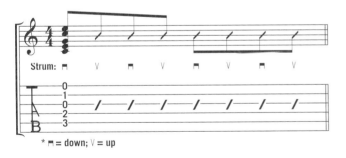

In music played with the pick-hand fingers, *split stems* are often used to highlight the division between thumb and fingers. With split stems, notes played by the thumb have stems pointing down, while notes played by the fingers have stems pointing up. If split stems are not used, pick-hand fingerings are usually present. Here is the same fingerpicking pattern shown with and without split stems. Clarity will inform which option is used.

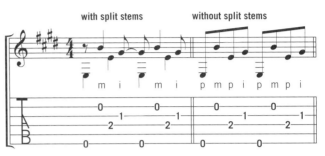

## CHORD DIAGRAMS

Chord diagrams are a convenient way of depicting chord shapes. Frets are presented horizontally. The thick top line represents the nut. A fret number to the right of a diagram indicates a chord played higher up the neck (in this case the top horizontal line is thin and the fret number is designated). Strings are shown as vertical lines. The line on the far left represents the sixth (lowest) string, and the line on the far right represents the first (highest) string. Dots mark where the fingers go, and thick horizontal lines illustrate barres. Numbers above the diagram are fretting-hand finger numbers, as used in standard notation.

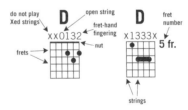

The given fingerings are only suggestions. They are generally what would most typically be considered standard. In context, however, musical passages may benefit from other fingerings for smoothest chord transitions. An X means a string that should be muted or not played; 0 indicates an open string.

## CAPOS

If a capo is used, a Roman numeral designates the fret where the capo should be placed. The standard notation and tablature is written as if the capo were the nut of the guitar. For instance, a tune capoed anywhere up the neck and played using key-of-G chord shapes and fingerings will be written in the key of G. Likewise, open strings held down by the capo are written as open strings.

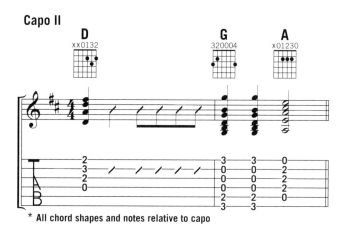

\* All chord shapes and notes relative to capo

## TUNINGS

Alternate tunings are given from the lowest (sixth) string to the highest (first) string. D A D G B E is standard tuning with the bottom string dropped to D. Standard notation for songs in alternate tunings always reflects the actual pitches of the notes.

## VOCAL TUNES

Vocal tunes are sometimes written with a fully tabbed-out introduction and a vocal melody with chord diagrams for the rest of the piece. The tab intro is usually your clue as to which strumming or fingerpicking pattern to use in the rest of the piece. The melody with lyrics underneath is that which is sung by the vocalist. Occasionally, smaller notes are written with the melody to indicate other instruments or the harmony part sung by another vocalist. These are not to be confused with cue notes, which are small notes that express variation in melodies when a section is repeated. Listen to a recording of the piece to get a feel for the guitar accompaniment and to hear the singing if you aren't skilled at reading vocal melodies.

## ARTICULATIONS

There are a number of ways you can articulate a note on the guitar. Notes connected with slurs (not to be confused with ties) in the tablature or standard notation are executed with either a hammer-on, pull-off, or slide. Lower notes slurred to higher notes are played as hammer-ons; higher notes slurred to lower notes are played as pull-offs.

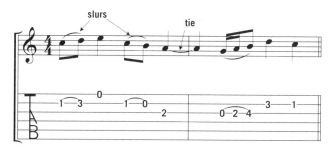

Slides are represented with dashes. A dash preceding a note is a slide into the note from an indefinite point in the direction of the slide; a dash following a note is a slide off the note to an indefinite point in the direction of the slide. For two slurred notes connected with a slide, pick the first note and then slide into the second.

Bends are denoted with upward arrows. Most bends have a specific destination pitch—the number above the bend symbol shows how much the bend raises the pitch: ¼ for a slight bend, ½ for a half step, 1 for a whole step.

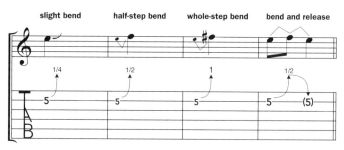

Grace notes are represented by small notes with a slash through the stem in standard notation and with small numbers in the tablature. A grace note is a quick musical ornament with no specific note value leading into a note, most commonly executed as a hammer-on, pull-off, or slide. In the first example below, pluck the note at the fifth fret on the beat, then quickly hammer onto the seventh fret. The second example is executed as a quick pull-off from the second fret to the open string. In the third example, both notes at the fifth fret are played simultaneously (even though it appears that the fourth string at the fifth fret is to be played by itself), then the fourth string, seventh fret is quickly hammered.

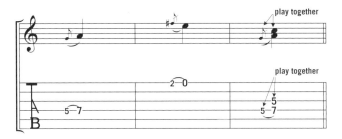

## HARMONICS

Harmonics are expressed as diamond-shaped notes in the standard notation and a small dot next to the tablature numbers. Natural harmonics are indicated with the text "Harmonics" or "Harm." above the tablature. Harmonics articulated with the picking hand (often called artificial harmonics) include the text "R.H. Harmonics" or "R.H. Harm." above the tab. Picking-hand harmonics are executed by lightly touching the harmonic node (usually 12 frets above the open string or fretted note) with the picking hand index finger and plucking the string with the thumb, ring finger, or pick. For extended phrases played with picking-hand harmonics, the fretted notes are shown in the tab along with instructions to touch the harmonics 12 frets above the notes.

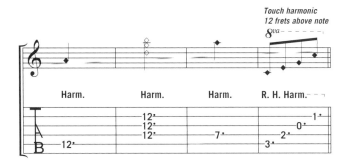

## REPEATS

One of the most confusing parts of a musical score can be the navigation symbols, such as repeats, *D.S. al Coda*, *D.C. al Fine*, *To Coda*, etc. Repeat symbols are placed at the beginning and end of the passage to be repeated.

When you encounter a repeat sign, take note of the location of the begin repeat symbol (with the dots to the right of the lines), play until you reach the end repeat symbol (with the dots to the left of the lines). Then go back to the begin repeat sign, and play the section again.

If you find an end repeat only sign, go back to the beginning of the piece and repeat. The next time you get to the end repeat, continue to the next section of the piece unless there is text that specifically indicates to repeat additional times.

A section will often have a different ending after each repeat. The example below includes a first and a second ending. Play until you hit the repeat symbol, return to the begin repeat symbol, and play until you reach the bracketed first ending. Then skip the measures under the bracket and jump immediately to the second ending, and then continue.

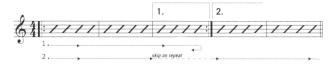

*D.S.* stands for *dal segno* or "from the sign." When you encounter this indication, advance immediately to the sign (𝄋). *D.S.* is usually accompanied by *al Fine* or *al Coda*. *Fine* indicates the end of a piece. A coda is a final passage near the end of a piece and is indicated with ⊕. *D.S. al Coda* simply tells you to go back to the sign and continue on until you are instructed to move to the coda, indicated with *To Coda* ⊕.

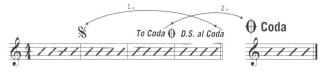

*D.C.* stands for *da capo* or "from the beginning." Jump to the top of the piece when you encounter this indication.

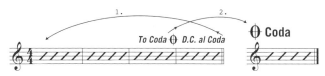

*D.C. al Fine* tells you to proceed to the beginning and continue until you encounter the *Fine* indicating the end of the piece (ignore the *Fine* the first time through).

Strumming through a waltz made
popular by the king of rock 'n' roll

# ARE YOU LONESOME TONIGHT?

"Are You Lonesome Tonight?" is best known today as an Elvis Presley song, but the tune actually goes back to the Roaring Twenties. Written in 1926 by Lou Handman and Roy Turk, it was a hit for a number of vocalists in the '20s and '30s—Vaughn De Leath, Henry Burr, Gene Austin, and others. The song saw another peak in popularity starting with Al Jolson's 1950 version, peaking ten years later with Presley's iconic rendition, which spent six weeks at No. 1 on the *Billboard* chart.

Recordings through the years have varied in both the style of the day and the arrangements. An intro section and a Shakespeare-inspired recitation have been used or set aside to suit each version. Presley's interpretation, for example, dropped the intro but used the recitation; others use the intro and not the recitation. For this arrangement, in the key of G major, we're going to concentrate on just the main body of the song.

We're going to keep things simple, with a relaxed tempo and mostly open chords. The arrangement runs through the song form twice, with the first ending landing on Daug (D F♯ A♯). Augmented chords hold a lot of tension and just ache to resolve back to the I chord (in this case, G), so they're a great device for this job. At the second ending, an E7 chord sets up a tag in which the last line is repeated. The E7, with its major third (G♯), adds a moment of brightness to lift us for the ending.

For the strumming, I would recommend a common waltz pattern—play a bass note on the first beat of each measure, followed by downward strums on the higher strings, squarely on beats 2 and 3. If you're playing a chord for more than two measures, such as the Em shown notated in the accompaniment pattern, try alternating the bass note—play the root (open low E) in the first bar and the fifth (B on string 5, fret 2) in the next measure. Be sure to strum gently, to best suit the character of this classic song.

11

**Accompaniment Pattern**

# THE BALLAD of CASEY JONES

## A classic railroad song about a real-life hero's tragic end

Not to be confused with the popular song by the Grateful Dead, "The Ballad of Casey Jones," also known as "Casey Jones, the Brave Engineer" or just "Casey Jones," is one of the great traditional American folk songs. Telling the story of Jones' death at the controls of the train he was driving, the song has built him into a mythical figure like Pecos Bill or Paul Bunyan. But Casey Jones was a real person, a highly respected train engineer with a reputation for always running on time.

The tragic accident memorialized in "Casey Jones" took place on the dark, foggy night of April 30, 1900, on the wet tracks outside of Vaughan, Mississippi. Rounding a long curve into that community at 75 miles per hour, Jones spotted the lights of a caboose stopped on the track ahead. He reversed his train's engine and slammed on its air brakes, managing to cut his speed to 45 m.p.h., but there wasn't enough track to stop. A few hundred feet before impact, the engineer told his fireman, Sim Webb, to jump. Jones managed to avert a potentially disastrous crash, saving the lives of the passengers but sacrificing his own.

Soon after the accident, an engine wiper named Wallace Saunders created a song about Jones and his demise, which he sang around the railroad yards to the tune of "Jimmie Jones," a popular song of the time. The song passed from person to person in the yards, and it evolved as it grew in popularity up and down the Illinois Central Line.

In 1909, a pair of vaudeville performers, T. Lawrence Seibert and Eddie Newton, published it with the title "Casey Jones, the Brave Engineer." Since then there have been dozens versions of the song—by Johnny Cash, Elizabeth Cotten, Pete Seeger, Jerry Garcia and others—with any number of alterations to the lyrics and form. The basic song is pretty simple, using just four chords, but many versions employ devices to keep its repetitive form moving, some with increasing tempos, and others changing keys.

My arrangement of "Casey Jones" starts out in the key of G major, with a modulation up to A, allowing me to keep everything in the friendly realm of simple open cowboy chording. It's best played at a moderate pace, for ease of singing—this is a rather wordy song! Of course, as always with this series, my expectation is that you will view this version as a starting point and do what feels interesting for you. If you're comfortable with barre chords, you could modulate every verse; if you're a fan of tongue twisters, you could gradually crank that tempo up like a runaway train down a mountainside. Try the song as a recitation. Make up your own lyrics. The point is to have fun with it.

15

THE BALLAD OF CASEY JONES

# BEAUTIFUL DREAMER

## Strumming through a classic by the 'father of American music'

"Beautiful Dreamer" was written by Stephen Foster (1826–1864)—often called the "father of American music"—at the end of his prolific career and published shortly after his untimely death. With its lilting rhythms and romantic lyrics, the song is one of America's most beloved serenades.

Although "Beautiful Dreamer" was popular long before the advent of recording or radio, Bing Crosby had a huge hit with it 1940. The tune was revived again in the 1960s, a full century after it was written, with artists like the Searchers and Billy J. Kramer with the Dakotas attempting to update the song for the youth market with a rock 'n' roll sound.

"Beautiful Dreamer" was originally written with piano accompaniment in the key of Eb major. Our arrangement transposes it to the more guitar-friendly key of C, with just a handful of chords, most of them open: C, Dm7, G, F, D7, and E. While most of these Campfire selections are in common (4/4) or waltz (3/4) time, "Beautiful Dreamer" is in 9/8—that's nine eighth notes per bar. Don't feel intimidated if you're

not familiar with this meter. If you play along with the video, you'll likely find that it's easy enough to channel the waltz-like feel.

I like to play the song with a fairly active accompaniment part. As shown in the verse pattern notated below, I tend to play a bass note followed by two strums, occasionally adding a walk-up for a bit of spice, as in the last measure. While I like to change bass notes to keep things interesting, you could stick on the same bass note for each chord—for instance, the third-fret C for the C chord and the open D for the Dm7 throughout.

For a two-bar intro, I use a figure based on the song's melodic hook, built around the C, F, and G chord shapes, and I play variations on it in other parts of the song over the G chord. If it's too difficult, feel free to omit it, but I would recommend working it up if you can, as it really makes the arrangement more engaging—and more fun to play—and that's what it's all about.

## Accompaniment Pattern

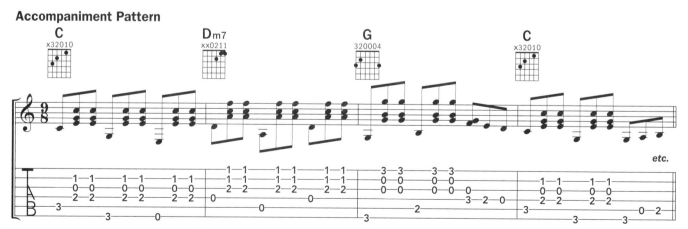

19

# DECK THE HALLS

## Yuletide evergreen with a country-and-western twinge

"Deck the Halls" is a traditional Christmas carol based on a Welsh carol dating back to the 16th century. The basic English lyric most everyone is familiar with today, written by the Scottish musician Thomas Oliphant (1799–1873), first appeared in 1862. Oliphant's original lyrics were a bit bawdy, with lines about flowing bowls, laughing, and quaffing. By 1877, a cleaned-up version, sans any mention of drinking, appeared in the *Philadelphia School Journal*, and rowdy lines like "Fill the mead cup, drain the barrel" had become the tame "Don we now our gay apparel."

Our campfire arrangement, like all in this book, uses just a few common, open chords—in order of appearance, C, F, G, Am7, and D7. For beginners, the F may be the most challenging of these formations, but this is as good a time as any to learn this essential chord shape. Playing the F as a full barre chord unlocks chords all the way up the neck, but there are some convenient workarounds. One solution, which I use a lot, is to wrap your thumb around the neck to fret the F on string 6, fret 1, instead of using the full barre shape. This is also a very efficient fingering, allowing for an easy transition between open shapes such as C and G.

I play the song with a simple boom-chuck strum pattern. As shown in the notation, pick a chord's root or fifth on beats 1 and 3 and strum the upper strings on 2 and 4. But most important, go for an energetic and festive feel.

**Basic Strumming Pattern**

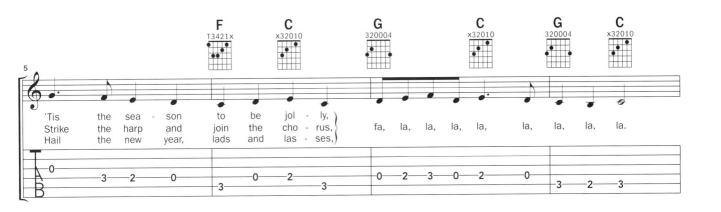

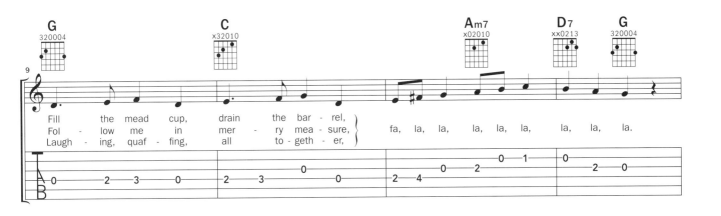

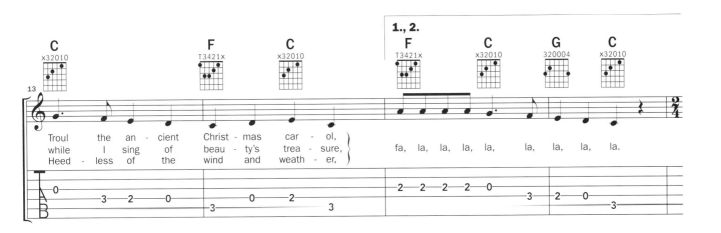

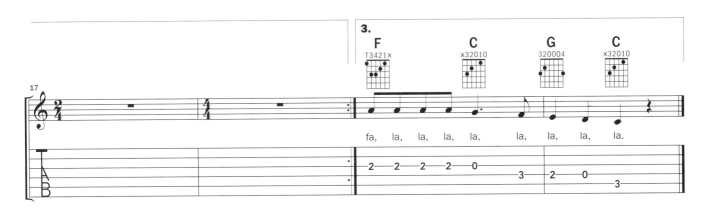

## Maintaining discipline on board with three simple chords
# DRUNKEN SAILOR

**G**enerally speaking, sea shanties are 19th-century shipboard work songs that are descendants of two primary sources: either the 18th-century work chants and sing-outs used by English and French sailors to coordinate certain tasks that required unanimous team effort or the traditional work songs sung by African and African-American laborers. The era of sea shanties as we know them appeared shortly after the War of 1812; reached its peak as work songs on sailing ships in the 1870s; and died with the eventual switch to engine power, which required far less coordinated manual labor on deck.

"Drunken Sailor," aka "Up She Rises," is one of the best-known sea shanties still in circulation. There's not

a lot to learn with this classic tune. With a light amount of digging you can find some more ornate arrangements, but our campfire version is the traditional, simple four-bar pattern using just three chords: Am, G, and C. The heart of this song is in the joy of group singing and the colorful, early morning treatments the singers are suggesting for their compromised colleague.

My arrangement includes a few of the more familiar verses, but this is a song that has had centuries to develop variations and alternate lyrics. Vary as they may, they generally stick to a theme of making crew members think carefully about returning from shore with any number of their sheets to the wind. So, what shall we do with a drunken sailor?

3. Put him in the hole with the *captain's daughter
   Put him in the hole with the captain's daughter
   Put him in the hole with the captain's daughter
   Early in the morning

*Captain's daughter is the nickname for the cat o' nine tails,
a whip made of knotted cords and used for corporeal punishment.

# HOME ON THE RANGE

## Strumming a Western classic with five easy chords

Of all the songs we'll look at here, "Home on the Range" is one of the most definitive examples of the classic campfire song. Originally based on the poem "My Western Home," written in 1872 by Brewster M. Higley, it was later turned it into the song we know today by Daniel E. Kelley.

Musicologist and folklorist John Lomax learned "Home on the Range" from a saloonkeeper in 1908 and published it in his *Cowboy Songs and Other Frontier Ballads* in 1910. Twenty-five years later, Bing Crosby released the recording that would become the standard for all the versions to follow. Obviously an easy fit for the cowboy stars of the day, such as Gene Autry, "Home on the Range" has also been recorded by quite

an array of pop and folk singers, from Frank Sinatra to Pete Seeger and Connie Francis to Tori Amos, making it one of the great pieces of classic Americana.

The song, like many of these old songs from before the advent of recording, has seen a number of variations, addition and omissions to the lyrics over the years. We'll work with a simple three-verse version in the guitar-friendly key of E major, using, with one exception, open chording.

The strumming pattern is a basic 3/4-time variety: the root (bass note) on the first beat and the higher strings on beats 2 and 3. This may be the most appropriate song you'll ever play when you're camping out under the stars.

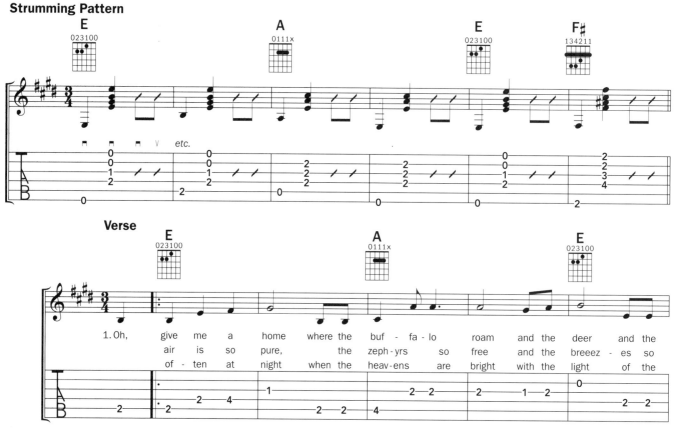

# The HOUSE of the RISING SUN

## How to strum along with a classic cautionary tale

The term "campfire song" is generally used to refer to a familiar old song that folks can sing along with to a simple guitar accompaniment. But the tunes we cover in this series extend beyond the repertoire of well-fed cowboys on the open range. Regardless of whether you're indoors or out, or how you cook your dinner, we call them campfire songs. As a singer-songwriter, I find learning these tunes and their history very interesting.

This selection, "The House of the Rising Sun," is a cautionary tale of things gone wrong in New Orleans. Made popular by a rock version that the Animals recorded in 1964, it has been a staple in folk music stretching back to at least the beginning of the 20th century, with roots in much older European folk traditions. While the basic melody was nailed down pretty early, the accompanying chords have seen a lot of variations along the way. The earliest recordings of the song—like Clarence Ashley and Gwen Foster's 1933 "Rising Sun Blues" and Woody Guthrie's version from 1941—were generally in

Appalachian folk or bluesy styles. Among my favorite other interpretations are Josh White's brooding solo take and Ronnie Gilbert's jazzy three-piece arrangement with the Weavers.

As always with the songs in this book, we'll keep the arrangement simple and stick with chords in open and first position: Am, then C with a G in the bass, D with an F# in the bass, and F (fretted with a full barre, which creates a neat descending bass pattern (A, G, F#, F). The only other chords are basic open C and E shapes.

The song is in 6/8 time—that's six eighth notes per bar, counted, "One, two, three, four, five, six." If you are not familiar with this meter, play along with the video to get a good sense of how it feels. I like to play the song with a flatpick, mixing things up with strums and single notes, as transcribed in the first eight measures. You could keep things even simpler and go with straight strumming throughout, or use a basic fingerpicking pattern—whatever works best for you.

**Intro/Strumming Pattern**

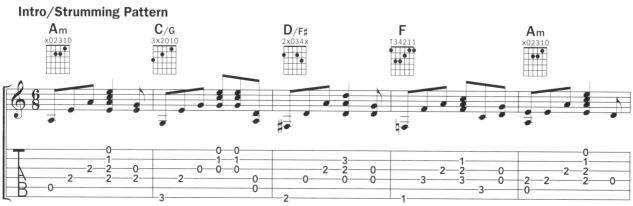

2. My mother was a tailor
   She sewed my new blue jeans
   My father was a gambling man
   Down in New Orleans

3. Now the only thing a gambler needs
   Is a suitcase and a trunk
   And the only time that he's satisfied
   Is when he's on a drunk

4. So, mother, tell your children
   Not to do what I have done
   Spend your lives in sin and misery
   In the House of the Rising Sun

5. Well, I got one foot on the platform
   And the other foot on the train
   I'm goin' back to New Orleans
   To wear that ball and chain

# I'M SITTING ON TOP OF THE WORLD

## A relaxed arrangement of a Roaring Twenties classic

There are a number of songs with titles similar to "I'm Sitting on Top of the World," perhaps the most famous of which is the country-blues number first recorded by the Mississippi Sheiks in 1930 and subsequently covered by a long list of musicians from Bob Wills and His Texas Playboys to the Grateful Dead to Jack White. In this lesson, I'll be covering a song that predates that example by a good five years.

This instance of "I'm Sitting on Top of the World" was written by Ray Henderson and lyricists Sam M. Lewis and Joe Young and published in 1925. Al Jolson's recording from that same year was the first major hit version for the song, but many other notable interpretations have been made over the years. My favorite version is Aretha Franklin's swinging arrangement from 1962.

To keep things accessible to players of all levels, this arrangement is taken at a relaxed tempo, using a handful of open and first-position chords—C, F, A7, D7, G7—along with a couple more sophisticated but easy-to-play shapes, F#dim7 and B♭9.

To play "I'm Sitting on Top of the World," I use a common fingerpicking pattern with an alternating bass, but you could also try strumming it with a pick, or, for that old-timey sound, using palm muting and a low G on the C chord. Both approaches are shown here in notation. Choose whichever works best for you, or mix and match the techniques. Note that I also like to include walk-ups (or walk-downs) on the bass strings here and there; these are shown with down-stemmed notes in the notation.

Do learn this arrangement as written, but my intent is that you will use this as a launching point for the song, so play around with it to find a tempo and rhythm that feels good to you.

31

# IT HAD TO BE YOU

**A guitar-friendly arrangement of a favorite
from the Great American Songbook**

"It Had To Be You" is one of the most popular and romantic tunes in the Great American Songbook. Written by the team of composer Isham Jones and lyricist Gus Kahn in 1924, its first recording by the Isham Jones Orchestra was a huge hit, staying at number #1 on the charts for five weeks. Since then, "It Had To Be You" has been recorded countless times and heard in many films and television shows.

"It Had To Be You" is also one of the more sophisticated selections in our campfire repertoire, but while there are nine chords used in this arrangement, they are all relatively simple forms that will be approachable by players who have the basic cowboy chords already under their fingers.

In order of appearance, the chords we'll use are Cmaj7, A7, D7, Am7, G7, E7, Fmaj7, Fm7, and Dm7. If you're new to these seventh chords, don't let them intimidate you—many of them require fewer fingers than their plain triad versions! The only barre chord is the Fm7, and that is among the easiest of all barre formations.

The strum I use here is a sort of loping, shuffle pattern. It resembles the standard boom-chuck rhythm, with the alternating bass pattern between two strings on beats 1 and 3 (the booms), and the rest of the chords on beats 2 and 4 (chucks). But the bounce comes from the light upstrokes between the booms and chucks.

All in all, it's a rather easy play for a rather sophisticated song. Take it slow. And the first time you sing a little of "It Had To Be You" to that someone special, every bit of the work will be worth it!

*C'est très romantique!*

## Strumming Patterns

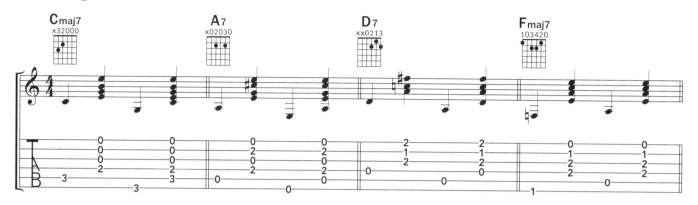

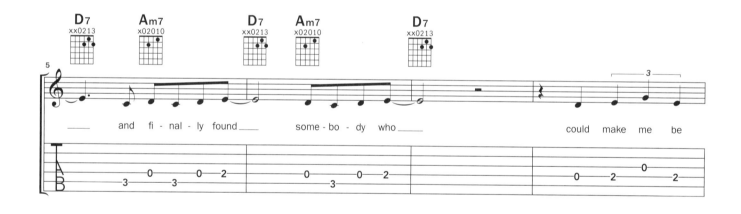

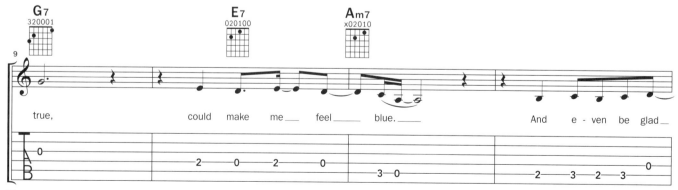

## A fun and breezy song dating back to the early 1800s
# JENNY JENKINS

**B**ack in the days before radio, recorded music, and DJs for hire, social gatherings such as quilting bees and church functions often featured fun interactive tunes where young people could safely socialize with each other. Dating back to at least the early 1800s, "Jenny Jenkins" is one of these dialogue songs, a vehicle for a boy to ask a girl to dance. The boy would sing the first lines, picking a color, and the girl would have to make up a response that rhymed. If she couldn't come up with a rhyme, she would dance with the boy.

"Jenny Jenkins," which has been covered by the likes of Jerry Garcia (with David Grisman) and Lisa Loeb, is as simple as it is sweet. I've arranged here it in the guitar-friendly key of D major using just three chords, including the common open D and G shapes.

Instead of a regular open A, I play a more colorful-sounding A7sus4—an A7 chord with the fourth (D) replacing the third (C#). These three voicings share the common note D (string 2, fret 3), which rings throughout for a lovely droning effect.

As for the picking hand, I start the song with a light boom-chuck, playing single bass notes on beats 1 and 3 and upper-string chord strums on beats 2 and 4, like notated here in the song's four bar intro. As seen in the accompanying video, I use that same pattern throughout.

With the boy-girl dialogue of "Jenny Jenkins" in mind—and through the magic of modern picture-in-picture technology—I had my friend Margaret Belton join me to respond to my relentless grilling regarding her wardrobe plans. Roll, Jenny Jenkins, roll!

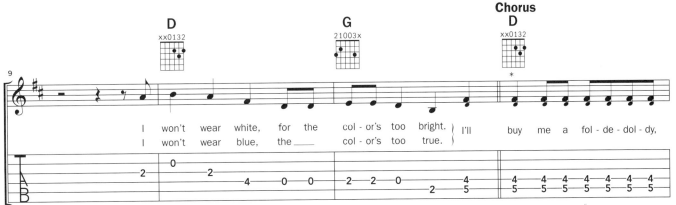

*In the video, the F♯ is sometimes sung as E through the first half of bar 14.*

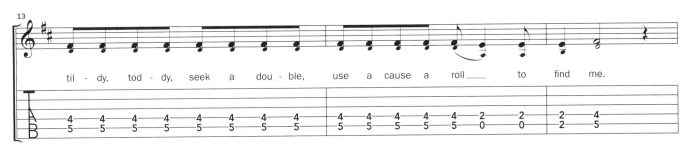

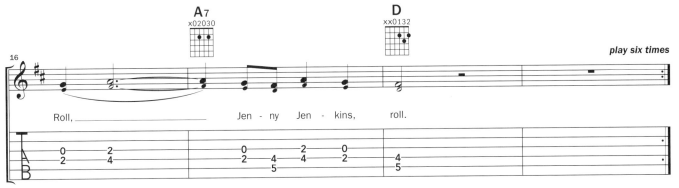

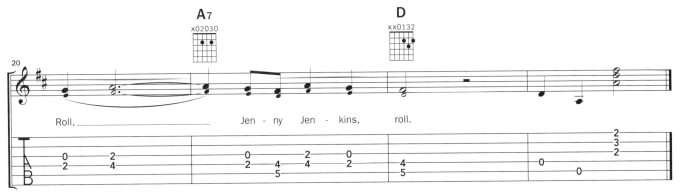

3. Will you wear red, oh my dear, oh my dear
   Will you wear red, Jenny Jenkins?
   I won't wear red, it's the color of my head

4. Will you wear black, oh my dear, oh my dear
   Will you wear black, Jenny Jenkins?
   I won't wear black, it's the color of my back

5. Will you wear green, oh my dear, oh my dear
   Will you wear green, Jenny Jenkins?
   I won't wear green, for it's a shame to be seen

6. So what will you wear, oh my dear, oh my dear
   What will you wear, Jenny Jenkins?
   Oh I'll just go bare with a ribbon in my hair

## A four-chord tribute to an American folk hero

# JOHN HENRY

The legend of the American folk hero John Henry is said to be based on a real man, but the facts behind the legend are clouded. It has been said that he was a steel driver who died when his heart gave out in a contest with a then-new, steam-powered drilling machine. The dates, location, and cause of his death are all the subject of debate, but we never let the details get in the way of a great traditional folk song. This enduring ballad stands as a tribute to human strength, endurance, and dignity versus the technology of the machine. It shines a light on the exploited labor of the industrial age and the shadows of slavery.

Songs featuring the story of John Henry are among the most recorded the American folk cannon, while being widely portrayed in film, television and literature. For this arrangement, we'll use four chords: G5, D5/F#, Em, and C. Chords with 5 as a suffix are variations that omit the major or minor third from the basic three-note triad. This produces a very strong, harmonically stable sound. The G5 I use here includes the D on string 2, fret 3, in place of the open B (the major third) often used in the open-G form. I avoid the first string altogether for this voicing.

For the D5/F#, I play the F# with my second finger. I like this formation, as adding the F# to the bottom adds a fullness to the sound and makes for a smooth descending bass line in the G5–D5/F#–Em progression. Additionally, that shared D on the third fret of the second string adds a nice ring through the changes.

"John Henry" has been played with all sorts of rhythmic approaches from hyper bluegrass tempos to easy listening. You could do this with simple strumming, but for this version I'm using a basic Travis-picking pattern, as shown here in notation, with the thumb picking steady quarter notes on the bass strings, while the other fingers add notes on the higher strings. This approach adds a nice syncopated bounce.

**Accompaniment Patterns**

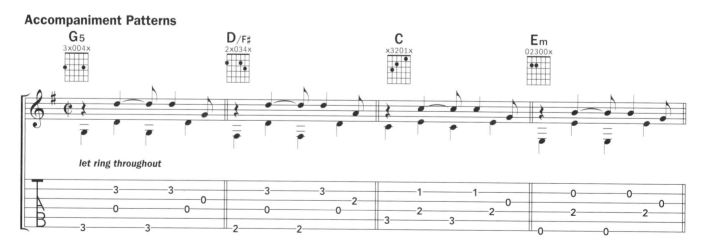

**Verse**

1. When John Henry was a little baby,
   captain said to John Henry, "I'm

sit-tin' on his dad-dy's knee, he
gon-na bring that steel drill a-round. I'm

picked up a ham-mer and a piece of steel and cried, "This
gon-na bring that steel drill out on these tracks. I'm gon-na

ham-mer's gon-na be the death of me, Lord, Lord. This
lay that steel on down, Lord, Lord. I'm gon-na

*Maurice Tani sings the C an octave below.*

39

*Maurice Tani sings the C an octave below.

3. Well John Henry told his captain,
   "Lord, a man ain't nothin' but a man
   But before I let that steam drill beat me
   I'll die with a hammer in my hand, Lord, Lord
   I'll die with a hammer in my hand"

4. Well John Henry drivin' on the right side
   That steam drill drivin' on the left
   He said, "Before I let your steam drill beat me
   I'll hammer myself to death, Lord, Lord
   I'll hammer my fool self to death"

5. Well John Henry said to his shaker,
   "Shaker, why don't you sing?
   'Cause I'm swingin' 30 pounds from my hips on down
   Yeah listenin' to my cold steel ring, Lord, Lord
   Listenin' to my cold steel ring"

6. Well the captain, he said to John Henry
   "What is that storm I hear?"
   John Henry said, "That ain't no storm, captain
   That's just my hammer in the air, Lord, Lord
   That's just my hammer in the air"

7. John Henry hammered in the mountains
   His hammer was strikin' fire
   But he worked so hard it broke his heart
   John Henry laid down his hammer and he died, Lord, Lord
   He laid down his hammer and he died

8. Well now John Henry, he had him a woman
   By the name of Polly Ann
   She walked out to those tracks, picked up John Henry's hammer
   Polly drove steel like a man, Lord, Lord
   She drove steel like a man

9. Well the captain called for a measure
   So they brought out a tape so fine
   Human hands laid down 12 feet of hard track
   And that steam drill laid just nine, Lord, Lord
   That steam drill laid just nine

10. They took John Henry to the graveyard
    They laid him in the sand
    Every locomotive car a-rollin' on by
    Hollered, "There lies a steel-drivin' man, Lord, Lord
    There lies a steel drivin' man"

11. Now every Monday mornin'
    When the bluebird begins to sing
    You can hear John Henry from a mile or more,
    You can hear John Henry's hammer ring, Lord, Lord
    You can hear John Henry's hammer ring

# LET ME CALL YOU SWEETHEART

## Cowboy chords with a hint of jazz sophistication

"Let Me Call You Sweetheart" has been an enduringly popular staple of the American songbook since it first appeared over 100 years ago. Written by the team of composer Leo Friedman and lyricist Beth Slater Whitson, the song was a huge hit for the Peerless Quartet in 1911. It has since been recorded countless times, by such popular artists as Pat Boone, Fats Domino, Bing Crosby, and the Mills Brother. The Peerless Quartet's recording was selected by the Library of Congress in 2015 for the National Recording Registry as "culturally, historically, or aesthetically significant."

Originally having an introductory verse section, most popular versions since Crosby's rendition (recorded first 1934 and then again in 1944) have consisted of simply the chorus repeated, often with an instrumental interlude in between.

That's the arrangement we're going to work with for our campfire version.

As usual, we're going to stick with cowboy chords—open A, D, and B7—but we'll spice it up with a couple of more adventurous chords: Bdim7 and Cdim7. These are essentially the same formation, placed a fret apart from each other. Lastly, we have an F#, which is commonly played as a barre chord, but as I often do with this formation, I wrap my thumb around the top of the neck to catch the root of the chord on string 6, fret 2.

The strumming part is pretty simple—just play a bass note on beat 1 of each bar, followed by strums on 2 and 3. If you'd like, add the occasional bass walk-up, as shown in the first measure here. With just a little practice, it should be easy enough to croon and strum this early 20th-century hit.

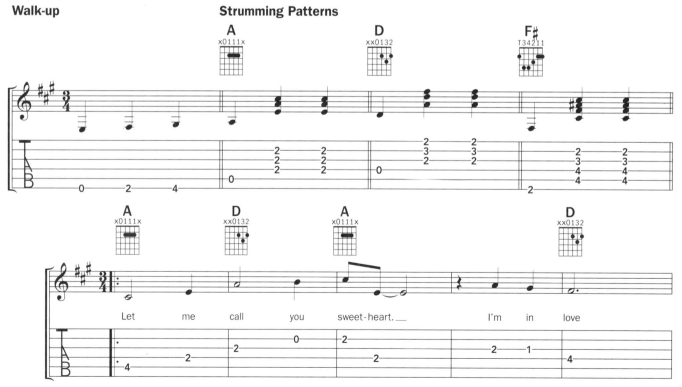

# LOW BRIDGE, EVERYBODY DOWN

## A nostalgic song about mule-powered barges of the 19th century

Dating way back to the early 1900s, "Low Bridge, Everybody Down" is well over a century old. The song takes a nostalgic look even farther back, to the mid-1800s, when traffic on the Upstate New York canal consisted mainly of barges towed by mules, eventually replaced by engine power. In 1912, when Thomas S. Allen wrote and recorded "Low Bridge," the Erie Canal was being absorbed into the New York State Barge Canal System and the era of mule power was romanticized with a longing for the good old days.

The popularity of "Low Bridge" came in two major waves, first in the early 20th century, through recordings by singers such as Billy Murray and Vernon Dalhart. In the postwar folk era that lasted well into the 1960s, versions by Pete Seeger, the Weavers, the Kingston Trio, and others made the song a folk staple.

For this arrangement I use a common boom-chuck strum pattern and simple open chords. The progression itself is relatively basic but has some cool touches. I particularly like the recurring sequence of chords—E–B7/F#–G–Em with a stepwise bass line motif (E to F# to G)—that's used throughout the song. It's no more difficult to play the B7 chord with the fifth (F#) rather than the root (B) in the bass in these passages, but it gives you a distinctive lifting movement that really draws the listener in.

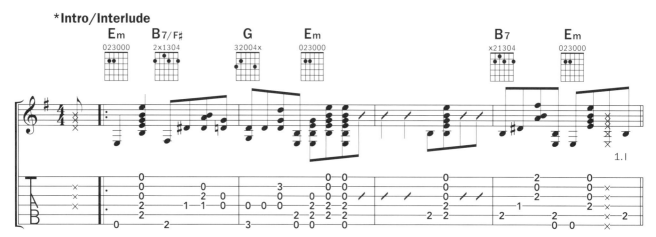

*On the video, Maurice Tani uses this four-bar chord sequence as an outro as well.*

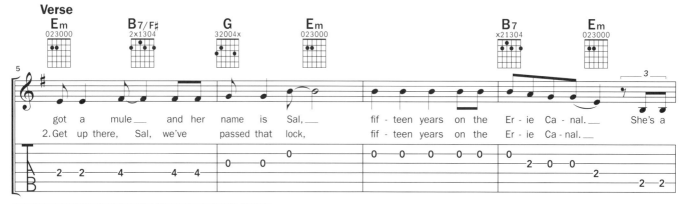

## Learn a streamlined arrangement of a Great American Songbook classic

# MANHATTAN

Written in 1922, "Manhattan" was the first hit for the songwriting team of Richard Rogers and Lorenz Hart, who would also compose other standards now considered part of the Great American Songbook, such as "Blue Moon," "My Funny Valentine," and "Where or When."

"Manhattan" is a great example of lyricist Hart's wry sense of humor. His protagonists are a young couple in love, low on money but rich in imagination when reframing their romantic travel aspirations as a frugal staycation in the city. Hart's joke here was that all the glamorous activities and locations mentioned in the song were really the cheapest, often grittiest attractions New York had to offer.

Popular versions of "Manhattan" have been recorded by the jazz singer Blossom Dearie, Motown act the Supremes, and many others. Arrangements tend to vary from one to three verses, both with and without an intro. I'm using a two-verse version with intro, similar to the version that jazz vocalist Ella Fitzgerald recorded on her album *Ella Fitzgerald Sings the Rodgers and Hart Song Book* (1956), slowing it down and moving it to the key of D major for ease of playing.

Some of the chords you're going to use are a bit more sophisticated than those typically seen in this column. And while a few have fancy names, they're all pretty easy to play—no major finger contortions required here. That said, it might at first be tricky to do the third-finger barre required for the F#>m7 and C9, B9, and Bb9 chords. Feel free to eliminate the highest note on the F#m7, and for C9 and B9, you could use an alternate shape: fingers 2, 1, 3, and 4 on strings 5, 4, 3, and 2, respectively, avoiding the notes on string 1.

Do take the time to appreciate the sounds that these chord types impart to the music—they really do add some spice.

**Intro Pattern**

**Verse Pattern**

**Intro**

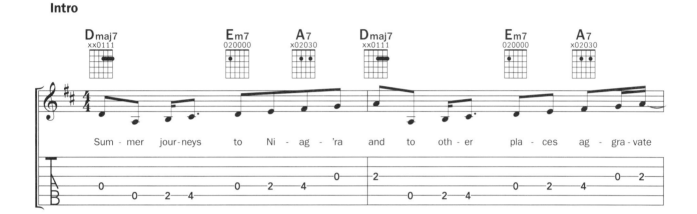

Sum - mer  jour - neys  to  Ni - ag - 'ra  and  to  oth - er  pla - ces  ag - gra - vate

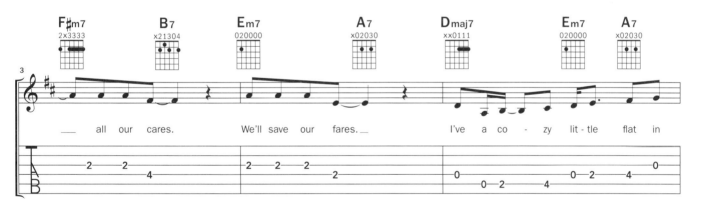

___ all  our  cares.  We'll  save  our  fares. ___  I've  a  co - zy  lit - tle  flat  in

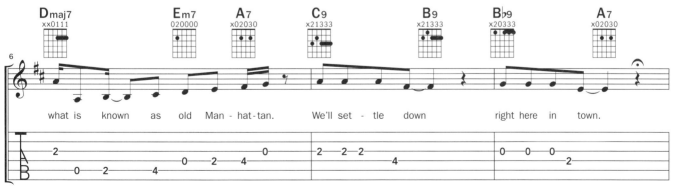

what  is  known  as  old  Man - hat - tan.  We'll  set - tle  down  right  here  in  town.

**Verse**

# MY BONNIE LIES OVER THE OCEAN

**Traditional Scottish folk song either about a war hero or a lost lover**

"My Bonnie Lies Over the Ocean" is a traditional Scottish folk song dating back to the mid-1800s, if not the 1700s. While the origin of the song is a bit murky, the original Bonnie is speculated to have been Charles Edward Stuart, aka Bonnie Prince Charlie. As leader of the Jacobite rising of 1745, his army was defeated by the British at the Battle of Culloden the following year. Stuart subsequently fled across the ocean from Scotland to France and over time became romanticized as a figure of heroic failure.

Of course, thanks to the ambiguous nature of the lyric, Bonnie could refer either to a man or woman, and the premise of the song could be interpreted as a love song as easily as historically rooted.

By the 1870s, "My Bonnie" had become popular with college and other singing groups on both sides of the Atlantic. Since then, it has regularly appeared in folk song collections and compilations. Its wide and long familiarity has also made it fertile ground for parody and updated versions, such as Tony Sheridan's rock 'n' roll arrangement with the Beatles.

As usual with these Campfire arrangements, I keep it simple, sticking to a handful of basic open chords: C, F, D7, A7, and G. But to keep things interesting I use a few twists—for instance, sometimes playing the C chord with a G in the bass, the D7 with an F♯ in the bass, and G6 (G B D E) rather than G (G B D).

For the strumming pattern, I use a classic waltz pattern—a bass note on beat 1, followed by strums on 2 and 3, all in downstrokes. Sometimes I throw in an upstroke strum on the "and" of beat 2 and/or 3. This helps keeps the proceedings lively.

**Strumming Pattern**

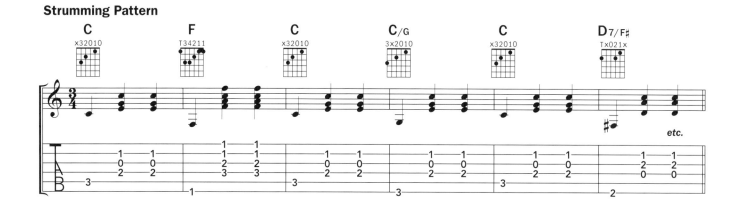

**Verse**

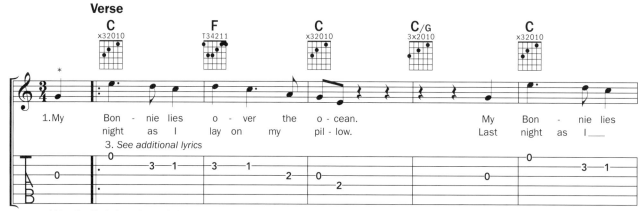

*Maurice Tani sings the melody an octave lower.*

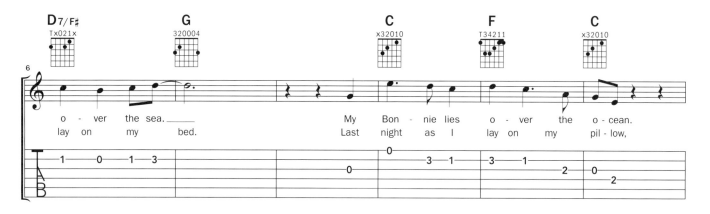

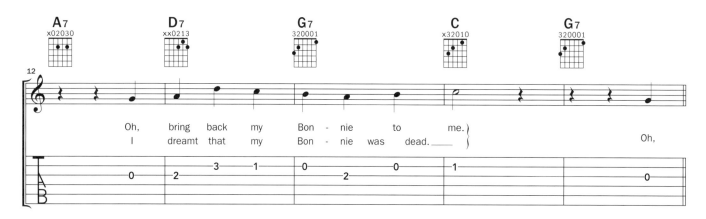

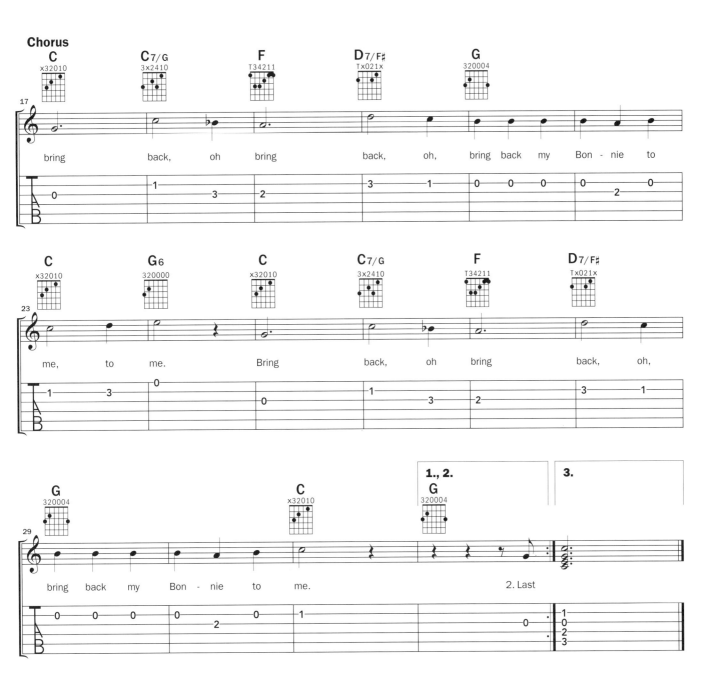

3. The winds have blown over the ocean
   The winds have blown over the sea
   The winds have blown over the ocean
   And brought back my Bonnie to me

## A classic North American folk song, arranged with rich details
# OH SHENANDOAH

"Oh Shenandoah" is a sea shanty–style folk song dating back to the early 19th century. The precise origin of the song is unclear, but it appears to have originated with fur traders making early contact with the various indigenous people in North America. Over time, the song developed multiple sets of lyrics as it made its way through sailors around the world. But the version we're most familiar with today tells the story of a canoe-going trader who wants to marry the daughter of a chief from an indigenous tribe. It is one of the great classics of American folk music and has been covered by everyone from Glen Campbell to Bob Dylan to Jerry Garcia

This arrangement is fairly straightforward, but I've added a few embellishments that set it apart from the most basic folk accompaniment and make it a bit more fun to play as a guitarist. Instead of a full open G chord, I'm using an alternative G5 shape. To keep this as clean as possible, I take care to deaden the A and high E strings. This way, only Gs and Ds ring, making

for a punchier sound without the added harmonic information of the chord's third (B).

To create more movement in the bass, I use two types of D chords, one a basic open shape, and the other with my second finger on the third (F#) on the low E string. This voicing lends an interesting tonality, fattens up the chord, and allows us to create a descending bass line through a progression of chords like G, D, and Em. Other chords I'm using include Em7 and A7sus4. Notice that nearly all of these chords maintain a constant D on the third fret of the second string, creating a distinctive drone in the treble side.

As for the right hand, I'm using a rather stoic fingerpicking pattern shown in the notation. I think of this as a piano-like approach—a dignified base for this dignified gem of old school Americana.

**Accompaniment Patterns**

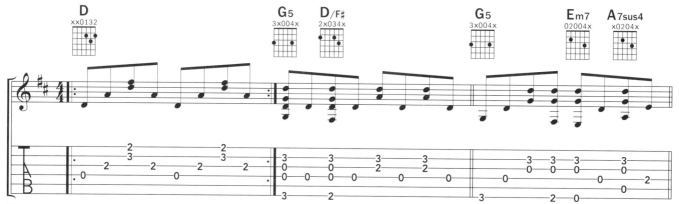

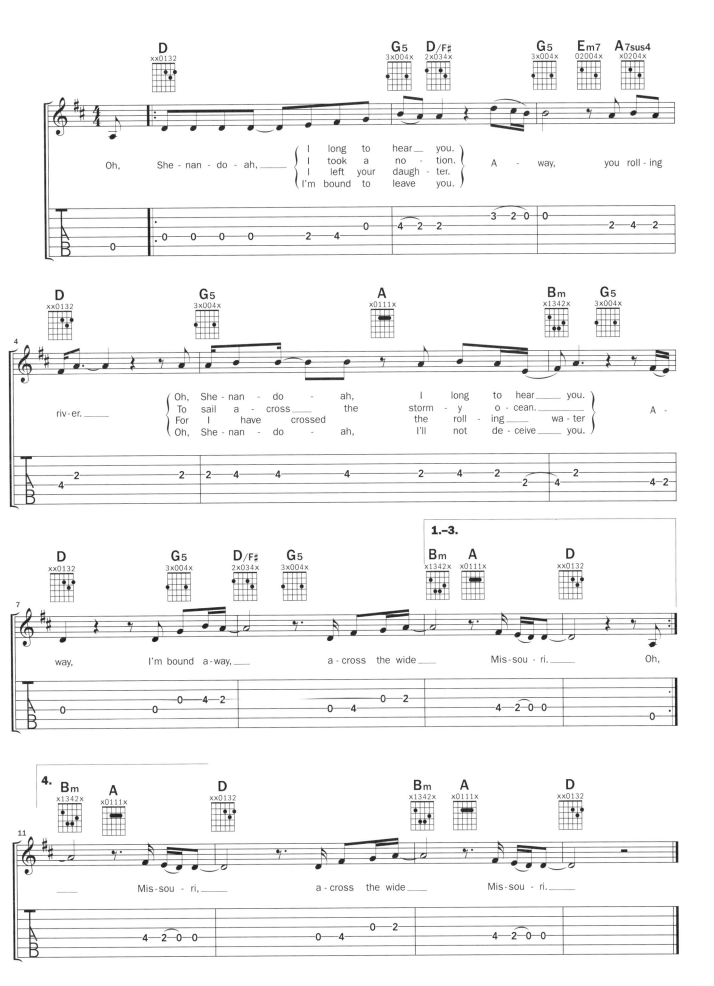

# ON TOP OF OLD SMOKY

## A fresh look at a centuries-old waltz

"On Top of Old Smoky" (sometimes spelled Smokey) is a traditional folk song with roots extending back to England, perhaps as long ago as the 16th century. It's a mournful, lonesome waltz with a sweet, lilting melody, and a lyric full of regret and bitterness.

Passed from generation to generation for centuries, "Old Smoky" has been recorded in a wide variety of styles by all sorts of artists—to name just a handful, Libby Holman, Pete Seeger, the Weavers (whose version reached the pop charts in 1951), Connie Francis, and Bruce Springsteen.

The song is customarily played with a simple three-chord progression, containing just the I, IV, and V chords, or C, F, and G, respectively, in the key of G major. That certainly gets the job done, but I like to do some harmonic embellishments. For instance, instead of just sticking with the C chord for the duration of bars 2–5, I add the relative minor chord, Am, in measure 4. I do the same thing with G and Em in bars 6–9. And in measure 10, instead of playing a regular open D chord, I add the third, F♯ in the bass, followed by a D7, also with a low note of F♯.

In terms of the picking hand, I use a classic waltz pattern: a bass note on beat 1 (either the root or the fifth of the chord), followed by downstroke strums on 2 and 3, sometimes with an upward strum added on the "and" of the beat. Little details like these, in tandem with my reharmonizations, help bring fresh color and anticipation to this old waltz.

**Intro/Strumming Pattern**

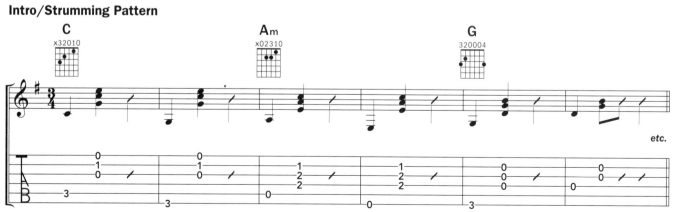

**Verse**

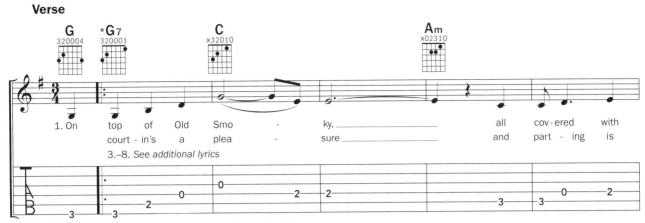

*\*First time only, play G chord instead of G7.*

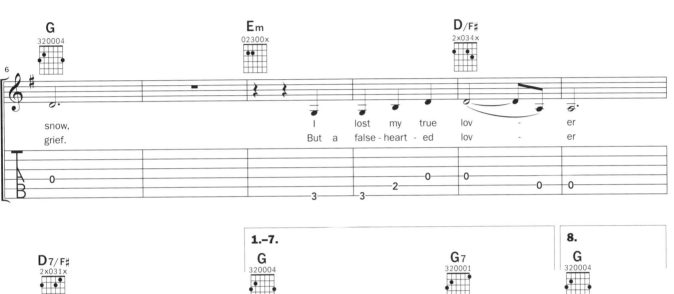

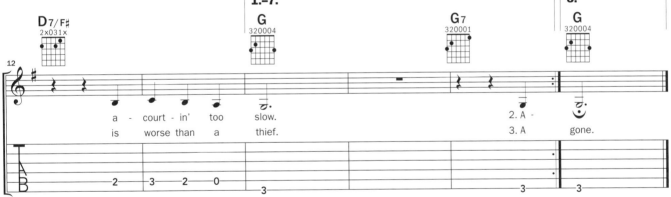

3. A thief he will rob you
   And take all you have
   But a false-hearted lover
   Will send you to your grave

4. And the grave will decay you
   And turn you to dust
   Not one girl in a hundred
   A poor boy can trust

5. They'll hug you and kiss you
   And tell you more lies
   Than the crossties on the railroad
   Or the stars in the skies

6. They'll tell you they love you
   Just to give your heart ease
   But the minute your back's turned
   They'll court whom they please

7. I'll go up on Smoky
   On the mountain so high
   Where the wild birds and the turtle doves
   Can hear my sad cry

8. And as sure as the dewdrops
   Fall on the green corn
   Last night she was with me
   Tonight she is gone

**Echoes of the American West from Brooklyn**

# RAGTIME COWBOY JOE

"Ragtime Cowboy Joe" is one of those quintessential classic western tune with roots nowhere near the great western expanse. Written by the Brooklyn team of Grant Clarke, Lewis F. Muir, and Maurice Abrahams, the song was inspired by the cowboy outfit of Abrahams' young nephew.

It was a huge hit around 1912 and has been recorded by many artists over the years, often in big band and Western swing styles with sophisticated chordal arrangements and sometimes furious tempos. But have no fear. This version is going to be easy to play—especially at a more moderate tempo.

I find this is a great song for beginners who have the basic chord shapes already under their fingers. While it's a bit more sophisticated than some of the other songs in this series, the chords are all simple open fare, and the longer form allows a guitarist to use a lot of the basic chords in one song. It's very satisfying to play for beginning and advanced musicians alike.

The chords are F, Dm, G7, C7, C, Am, E, and A7. The toughest for the beginner is usually the F. An easier method I use for getting a nice, full F chord is to wrap my thumb around the top of the neck to fret the sixth-string F rather than barring across all six strings. It isn't the best solution for every situation requiring an F, but this technique is a handy item to have in your bag of tricks.

As for the accompaniment pattern, I use a common boom-chuck pattern—bass notes on beats 1 and 3 and strums on 2 and 4. While generally played with a pick, I'm doing the pattern fingerstyle here. As always, I encourage you to learn the song like this, explore other versions, and then settle on a hybrid of your favorite aspects to create an arrangement that is your own.

**Accompaniment Patterns**

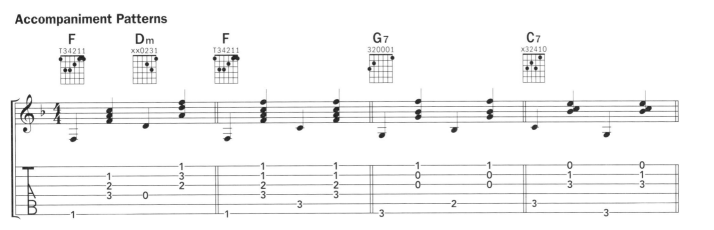

**Verse**
**Bouncy**

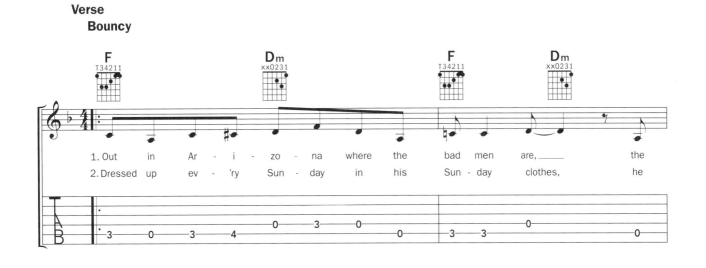

1. Out in Ar - i - zo - na where the bad men are, _____ the
2. Dressed up ev - 'ry Sun - day in his Sun - day clothes, he

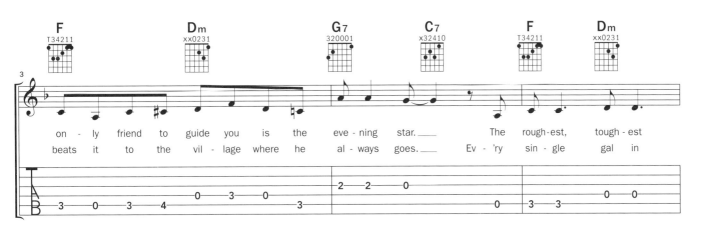

on - ly friend to guide you is the eve - ning star. _____ The rough - est, tough - est
beats it to the vil - lage where he al - ways goes. _____ Ev - 'ry sin - gle gal in

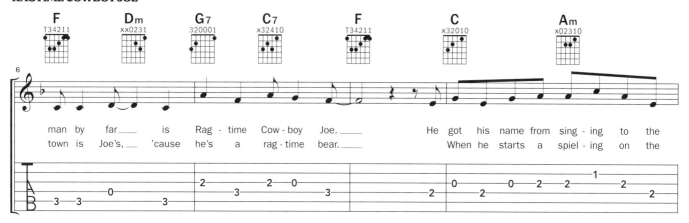

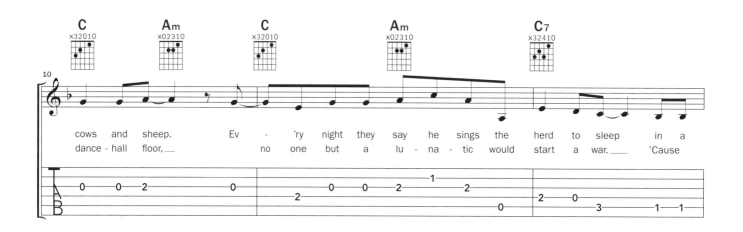

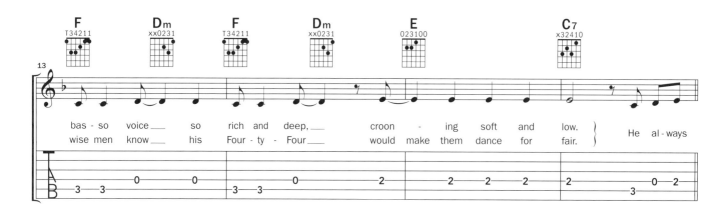

**Chorus**

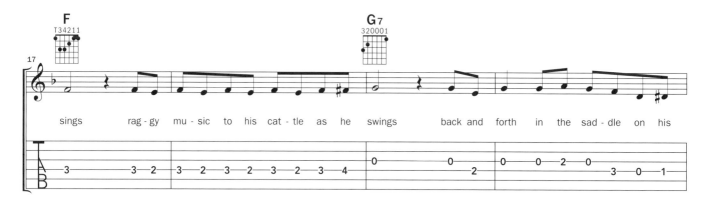

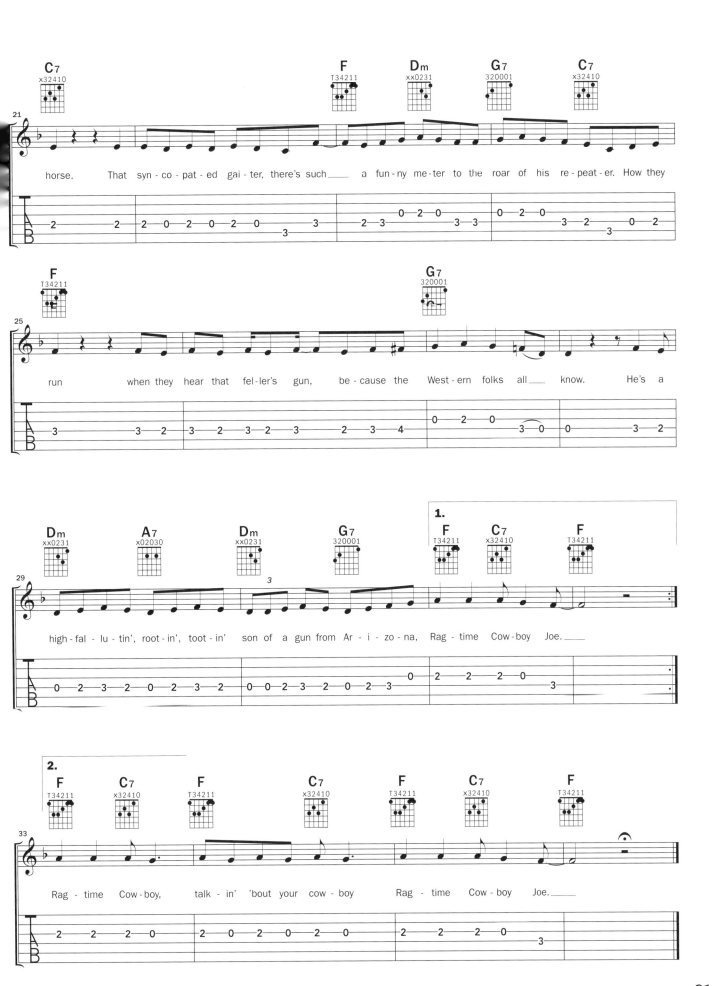

## An American cowboy classic
# RED RIVER VALLEY

"Red River Valley" is one of the best known tunes of the Old West—a classic campfire song in the most traditional definition. Of somewhat uncertain origin, this song dates back into the late 1800s, possibly written during the British Wolseley Expedition to Manitoba in the 1870s as a love song written by an indigenous Métis woman to a British soldier who was returning east.

Besides being one of the standards at summer camps, "Red River Valley" has appeared in many movies over the years as well having been recorded by artists as varied as Jimmie Rodgers, Woody Guthrie, Connie Francis, Bill Haley, Bing Crosby, Marty Robbins, the Ventures, and Bill Frisell.

With all those versions in the ever-evolving styles of the 100 years the song has been recorded, you'll be sure to find great variety in the approaches taken. But our simple campfire version of "Red River Valley" has a simple, repetitive chord pattern, using the I (C), IV (F), V (G), and I7 (C7) cowboy chords in the key of C major. The boom-chuck strumming pattern has a bouncy feel which I get just grazing the strings on the upstroke of the first eighth note of the chuck, and a common, alternating bass.

"Red River Valley" is a great place to start for beginners and an absolute must-have for those nights around the fire out under the stars.

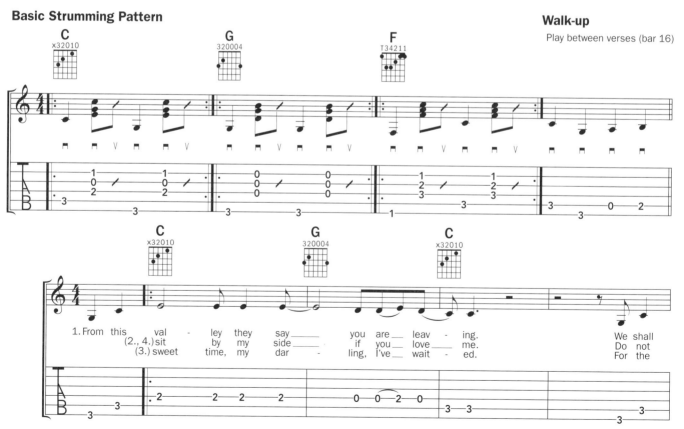

This arrangement copyright © 2020 String Letter Publishing.

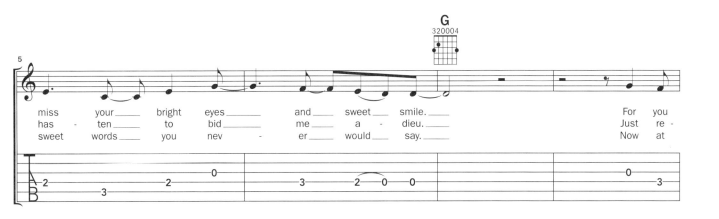

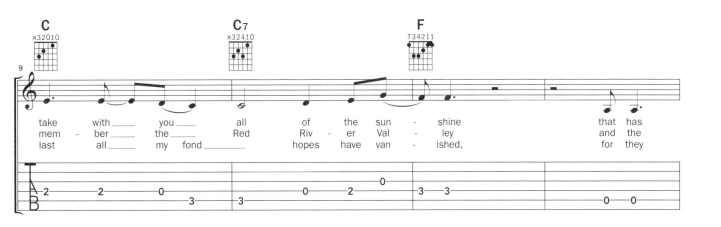

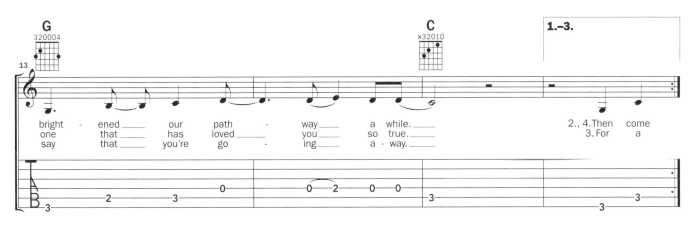

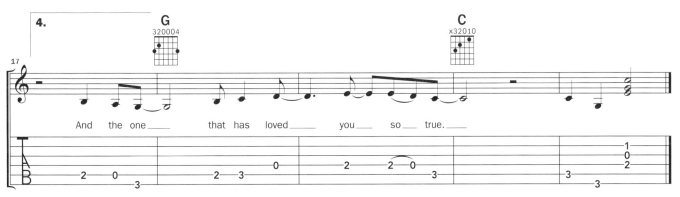

# A jug-band classic, popularized by the Grateful Dead and others

# STEALIN'

The great 1950s and '60s folk music wave saw a resurgence in popularity of 1920 and '30s jug band music, with artists of the day writing new material and reviving old, often obscure songs for younger generations. "Stealin'" is a perfect example and a fun, easy song to play.

First recorded by the New Orleans jazz musician Clarence Williams in 1921 as "Stealin' Stealin'," the most well-known version of the era was the 1928 recording by the Memphis Jug Band. "Stealin'," as it's alternatively titled, became a folk/pop standard through interpretations by the Grateful Dead, Bob Dylan, Dave Van Ronk, Arlo Guthrie, and others.

Like many folk and pop songs, "Stealin'" is built from the I, IV, and V chords—C, F, and G5, respectively, in the key of C major—with the vi chord (Am7) also thrown in. Note that the vocal line is somewhat

simplified in the notation, to make it more playable for guitarists of all abilities.

A couple tips for beginners: when strumming these cowboy chords, you don't need to play all of the strings. In this case, I omit the first string on all four chords, for a tighter sound. I also use efficient fingerings, which make it easier to switch between chords. For example, in bars 13 and 18, You can play the Am7 chord simply by removing your third finger from the C-chord shape.

For the strum, I use a basic boom-chuck pattern, with the occasional walk-up, shown here in notation. Note that for the C chord, with its alternating bass pattern, you'll need to move your third finger between the third fret on strings 5 and 6. Be sure to maintain a loose and relaxed strum throughout, for a kind of swinging feel, and you'll be stealin' back to your same old used to be!

## A great cowboy song, played with four cowboy chords

# STREETS OF LAREDO

It's very common to find that old, traditional songs were variations on other, even older traditional songs. In particular, melodies are often repurposed with a new set of lyrics. An example every American is familiar with—the national anthem—is based on the melody of a song sung after dinner in an ironically English gentlemen's club in the later 1700s. And one of the most iconic American cowboy songs, "The Streets of Laredo" originated in the late 1700s as an Irish ballad, "The Unfortunate Lad" (aka "The Unfortunate Rake").

Over the years, "Streets of Laredo" has seen lots of different recorded interpretations, by Johnny Cash, Joan Baez, and Chet Atkins, and other musical luminaries. The song is usually played with just four chords—the I, the IV, the V, and the V/V, or II—making it ideally suited for campfire play. For this arrangement, in the guitar-friendly key of C major, we're using the basic C (I), G (V), F (IV), and D (II) chords.

I use the strumming pattern shown here in the intro throughout the whole song. Basically, I pick a bass note on beat 1, followed by strums on 2 and 3. In the last measure of the intro, I play a little walk-up—G to A to B—that connects to the C chord at the start of the verse. I also use this walk-up for the last measure of the chorus (bar 74). Bass moves like this are a great way to add variety and movement to basic strumming patterns.

**Intro/Basic Accompaniment Pattern**

**𝄋 Verse**

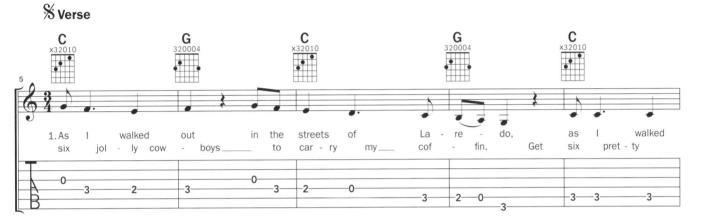

1. As I walked out in the streets of La - re - do, as I walked
six jol - ly cow - boys _____ to car - ry my _____ cof - fin. Get six pret - ty

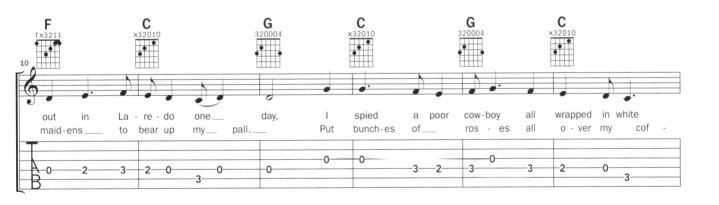

out in La - re - do one _____ day, I spied a poor cow - boy all wrapped in white
maid - ens _____ to bear up my _____ pall. Put bunch - es of _____ ros - es all o - ver my cof -

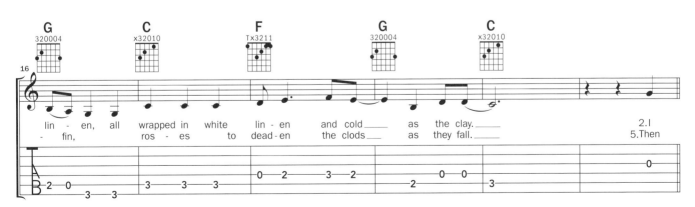

lin - en, all wrapped in white lin - en and cold _____ as the clay. _____
- fin, ros - es to dead - en the clods _____ as they fall. _____

2.I
5.Then

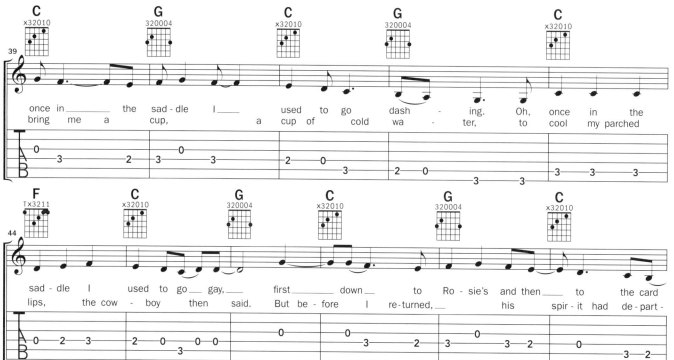

69

## Strumming through one of the great spirituals
# THIS LITTLE LIGHT OF MINE

"This Little Light of Mine" is one of those ubiquitous old gospel songs that has become such a part of the folk music tradition that it has transcended its roots as a spiritual and become the basis for secular versions by artists such as Ray Charles ("This Little Girl of Mine") and the Everly Brothers. It was adapted as something of an anthem for the Civil Rights Movement through the 1950s and '60s.

Hymnist Harry Dixon Loes is often credited as writing "This Little Light of Mine" as a children's song in the 1920s, but its origin is murky at best. Loes never claimed credit for the original version of the song, and the Moody Bible Institute where he worked said he did not write it. This is very common in traditional music where the songs have been passed down via word of mouth for many years and documentation only picks up when a folk musicologist comes along and records it.

"This Little Light of Mine" is nicely suited for campfire play. This arrangement is in the bright key of G major, with a handful of basic open chords. Note that in this version, I'm using a G5 chord (a G chord without its third, B). This makes for a lean and uncluttered sound that stands in contrast to the fuller G chord in the chorus/verse that follows. I also use a G7 chord in bar 8, but that is optional; you can just stay on a G chord here if you'd like. The G7 just gives the song a bit of color and anticipation to move along.

As for the accompaniment pattern, try using the common strumming pattern notated here. I'd advise you to worry less about playing what's written in the notation than aiming to hit the lower strings with a solid strum directly on beats 1 and 3, and the higher strings on 2 and 4. For this pattern, I use downward strums on all the beats, and upward strums on the "ands."

## A two-chord murder ballad from the hills of North Carolina
# TOM DOOLEY

The squeaky-clean cut image of the Kingston Trio seems almost incongruous with the very dark tale heard in their biggest hit, "Tom Dooley." This classic murder ballad tells the story of the death of Laura Foster at the hand of her lover, Tom Dula ( pronounced "Doo-lee"). It was a rather brutal crime that caught national attention for the extended trial and eventual execution of Dula on May 1, 1868.

The arrangement here is a bit of a mashup of the 1958 Kingston Trio hit, a recording by the country musician Bobby Ware, and various traditional versions dating back as far as 1929. Considering the song uses only two chords, this is a beginner-friendly selection—easy to play and familiar to many people.

In the key of F, the two chords we use are F and C7 (or the I and the V, respectively, in the key of F major).

If you're very new to the guitar, C may be among the first chords you learned, and you may well find F a bit challenging. (See "Deck the Halls" on page 17 for an easier alternative to the full barre chord shape shown here.) Try to be efficient when switching between F and C7—you may want to keep your third finger on the fifth-string C throughout, since that note is in both chords.

As with many of the other songs in this book, for accompaniment, I use the classic boom-chuck pattern—single bass notes on beats 1 and 3, and chords strums on 2 and 4—all with down- strokes. Though not indicated in the notation, I sometimes toss in an upstroke strum between the beats to add a little spring in Tom Dooley's step as he walks to that white oak tree.

**Intro/Basic Strumming Pattern**

## Chorus/Verse

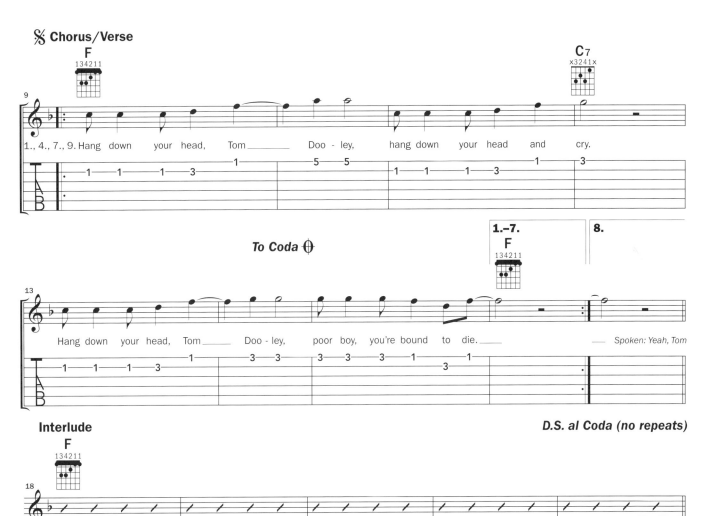

**To Coda** ⊕

*Spoken: Yeah, Tom*

**Interlude**

**D.S. al Coda (no repeats)**

*Dooley was hung for the murder of Laura Foster in Wilkes County, North Carolina, at sunrise on May 1, 1868.*

⊕ **Coda**

**N.C.**

poor    boy,    you're    bound    to    die.

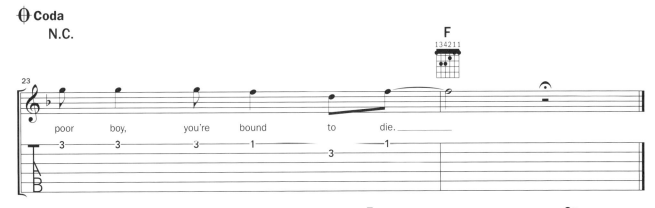

2. Met her on the mountain, there I took her life

Met her on the mountain, stabbed her with my knife

3. Took her on the hillside, God almighty knows

Took her on the hillside and that's where I hid her clothes

5. I dug a grave five feet long, I dug it three feet deep

Rolled the cold clay over her and stomped it with my feet

6. Baby, this time tomorrow, I reckon where I'll be

If it had not been for Grayson, I'd be here in Tennessee

8. This time tomorrow, reckon where I'll be

Down in some lonesome valley, hanging from a white oak tree

## A simple yet sophisticated arrangement of a popular waltz

# TONIGHT YOU BELONG TO ME

"Tonight You Belong to Me" is delightful 32-bar song that goes back to the Roaring Twenties. Written by Billy Rose and Lee David, it was a big hit for singer Gene Austin in 1926 as well as Roger Wolfe Kahn and others around the same time. The song began to pick up steam again in the early '50s when Frankie Laine recorded his sophisticated big band version, but the big hit was scored in 1956 with a version by the teen sister duo of Patience and Prudence, which hit No. 4 on the charts and sold over a million copies.

"Tonight You Belong to Me" has been recorded by many other artists since then, from Dottie West to Eddie Vedder and Cat Power. It has been heard in commercials, films, and television shows; Steve Martin and Bernadette Peters famously sang it in a charming scene in the 1979 comedy *The Jerk*.

As per our usual modus operandi, let's keep this arrangement simple and in a key (namely, D major) that allows for easy, primarily open chording. Though we're using more chords than usual—a total of nine, some of them jazzy—they're all pretty easy to form. Note the use of the Gm7 chord (G B♭ D F), which is borrowed from the key of D minor, adding a sophisticated flavor.

I like to fingerpick the simple accompaniment pattern shown here, but it will work just as well with a pick. Whichever technique you choose, be sure to play the song with a gently loping feel, as indicated by the swing eighth notes symbol at the beginning of the notation.

In other words, instead of playing two even notes per beat, play them long-short. If you are unsure how to do this, just follow along with the video.

**Accompaniment Pattern**

**An unlikely song makes for a satisfying but easy arrangement**

# WHAT'LL I DO

Irving Berlin was one of the giants of popular music in the 20th century, and his songs, musicals and film scores fill one of the largest slices of the Great American Songbook. Over his 60-year career, Berlin wrote hundreds of songs, many becoming major hits, including the scores for 20 original Broadway shows and 15 Hollywood movies that earned him eight Oscar nominations.

Berlin's 1923 romantic ballad "What'll I Do" has been recorded by artists in every decade—starting with Paul Whiteman in the '20s and continuing with the likes of Nat King Cole, Frank Sinatra, Judy Garland, Chet Baker, Linda Ronstadt, and Willie Nelson.

This campfire version is in the key of C major and features mostly open chords. It does start out with a mildly adventurous but easy to play Gaug (augmented) sound right at the top, but from there the chords are of the common cowboy variety. One of my favorite sounds in this song is the minor iv chord (Fm) that appears in the first bars of the verse. Used with the I (C major), the iv produces a longing tonality that is very appealing.

As I commonly do, for the F chord formations (F and Fm), I wrap my thumb over the top to play the root on the low string. I find the transition between the C, G and F formations easier and the fingering more efficient than barring all six strings. Simple fingerpicking patterns like the ones shown in notation help tie all the chords together in a smooth and flowing way that is befitting of such a beautiful ballad.

**Fingerpicking Patterns**

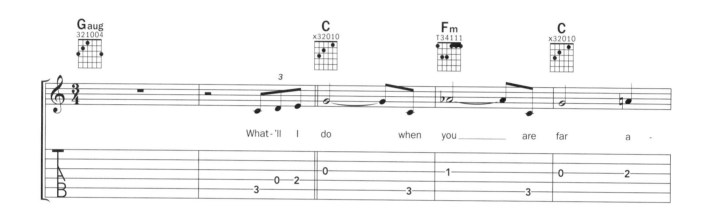

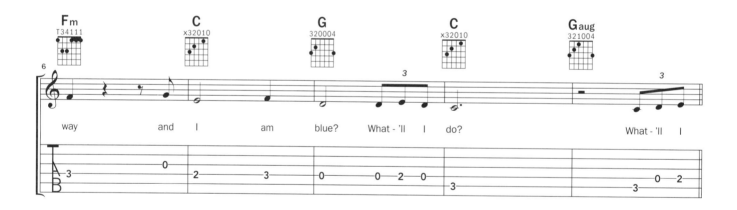

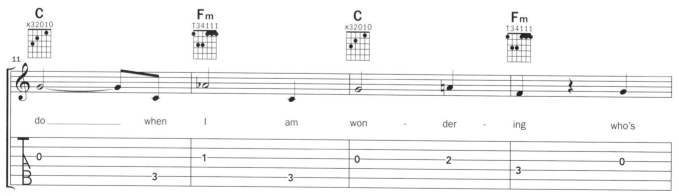

# ABOUT THE AUTHOR

Singer-songwriter and guitarist Maurice Tani (mauricetani.com) might hail from the West and rock a cowboy hat, but he's essentially a city boy—not really the sort one might expect to find crooning and strumming under the stars on the open range. But music is a great common denominator, a window where we see the world through different eyes, and campfire songs are natural fit in Tani's bulging scrapbook of styles.

Born and raised in San Francisco, Tani picked up the guitar as a teen and learned to play by reading through a Beatles songbook. He and a couple buddies then bashed it out with raw enthusiasm in the garage—psychedelic rock, California country, British Invasion—much to the dismay of the neighbors.

In college, Tani developed an interest in jazz and experimental electronic music and began playing professionally. A stint in Central Texas—playing five sets a night, seven nights a week, for months at a time in discos, hard rock clubs and some of the roughest country bars between Austin and Dallas—added new arrows to his quiver of styles.

A move to New York City at the beginning of the punk/art rock era, and then a return to touring and recording in California with ex-Flamin' Groovies rockin' frontman Roy Loney & the Phantom Movers expanded Tani's skill set further. He then spent 15 years touring with large dance bands.

Tani moved his primary focus back to his original music, initially based in electric California country, but gradually expanding to include many of the styles he had worked with over the years. He continues to pick up new influences as they reach his ear. His association with the Little Village record label and its extremely diverse roster of artists has proven to be a wellspring of inspiration, bringing blues, R&B, and deep gospel sounds to his mix.

In arranging campfire fare for acoustic guitar, Tani has found in these old songs yet another source of fresh influences that seep into his own work. Researching their histories and deconstructing them to present basic, simple, single-guitar arrangements has yielded new and valuable inspiration for his own writing, playing, and singing. He says, "Every one of these old, familiar songs has had something to teach me, which I have added to the pantry where I store my musical spices."